Visit Cram101.com for full Practice Exams

Textbook Outlines, Highlights, and Practice Quizzes

Visible Learning: A synthesis of over 800 meta-analyses relating to achievement

by John Hattie, 7th Edition

All "Just the Facts101" Material Written or Prepared by Cram101 Publishing

Title Page

Visit Cram101.com for full Practice Exams

WHY STOP HERE... THERE'S MORE ONLINE

With technology and experience, we've developed tools that make studying easier and efficient. Like this Cram101 textbook notebook, **Cram101.com** offers you the highlights from every chapter of your actual textbook. However, unlike this notebook, **Cram101.com** gives you practice tests for each of the chapters. You also get access to in-depth reference material for writing essays and papers.

By purchasing this book, you get 50% off the normal subscription free!. Just enter the promotional code **'DK73DW20745'** on the Cram101.com registration screen.

CRAM101.COM FEATURES:

Outlines & Highlights
Just like the ones in this notebook, but with links to additional information.

Integrated Note Taking
Add your class notes to the Cram101 notes, print them and maximize your study time.

Problem Solving
Step-by-step walk throughs for math, stats and other disciplines.

Practice Exams
Five different test taking formats for every chapter.

Easy Access
Study any of your books, on any computer, anywhere.

Unlimited Textbooks
All the features above for virtually all your textbooks, just add them to your account at no additional cost.

Be sure to use the promo code above when registering on Cram101.com to get 50% off your membership fees.

Visit Cram101.com for full Practice Exams

STUDYING MADE EASY

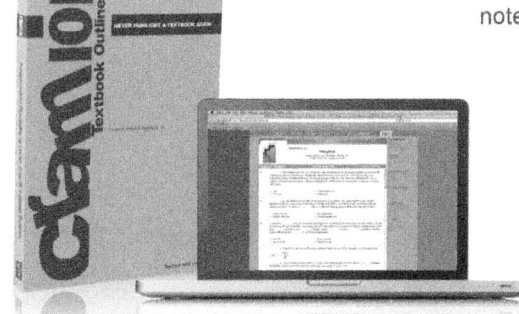

This Cram101 notebook is designed to make studying easier and increase your comprehension of the textbook material. Instead of starting with a blank notebook and trying to write down everything discussed in class lectures, you can use this Cram101 textbook notebook and annotate your notes along with the lecture.

Our goal is to give you the best tools for success.

For a supreme understanding of the course, pair your notebook with our online tools. Should you decide you prefer Cram101.com as your study tool,

we'd like to offer you a trade...

Our Trade In program is a simple way for us to keep our promise and provide you the best studying tools, regardless of where you purchased your Cram101 textbook notebook. As long as your notebook is in *Like New Condition**, you can send it back to us and we will immediately give you a Cram101.com account free for 120 days!

Let The *Trade In* Begin!

THREE SIMPLE STEPS TO TRADE:

1. Go to www.cram101.com/tradein and fill out the packing slip information.
2. Submit and print the packing slip and mail it in with your Cram101 textbook notebook.
3. Activate your account after you receive your email confirmation.

* Books must be returned in *Like New Condition*, meaning there is no damage to the book including, but not limited to; ripped or torn pages, markings or writing on pages, or folded / creased pages. Upon receiving the book, Cram101 will inspect it and reserves the right to terminate your free Cram101.com account and return your textbook notebook at the owners expense.

Visit Cram101.com for full Practice Exams

"Just the Facts101" is a Cram101 publication and tool designed to give you all the facts from your textbooks. Visit Cram101.com for the full practice test for each of your chapters for virtually any of your textbooks.

Cram101 has built custom study tools specific to your textbook. We provide all of the factual testable information and unlike traditional study guides, we will never send you back to your textbook for more information.

YOU WILL NEVER HAVE TO HIGHLIGHT A BOOK AGAIN!

Cram101 StudyGuides
All of the information in this StudyGuide is written specifically for your textbook. We include the key terms, places, people, and concepts... the information you can expect on your next exam!

Want to take a practice test?
Throughout each chapter of this StudyGuide you will find links to cram101.com where you can select specific chapters to take a complete test on, or you can subscribe and get practice tests for up to 12 of your textbooks, along with other exclusive cram101.com tools like problem solving labs and reference libraries.

Cram101.com
Only cram101.com gives you the outlines, highlights, and PRACTICE TESTS specific to your textbook. Cram101.com is an online application where you'll discover study tools designed to make the most of your limited study time.

By purchasing this book, you get 50% off the normal subscription free!. Just enter the promotional code **'DK73DW20745'** on the Cram101.com registration screen.

www.Cram101.com

Copyright © 2012 by Cram101, Inc. All rights reserved.
"Just the FACTS101"®, "Cram101"® and "Never Highlight a Book Again!"® are registered trademarks of Cram101, Inc.
ISBN(s): 9781478431862. PUBI-1.2012914

Learning System

facts101

Visible Learning: A synthesis of over 800 meta-analyses relating to achievement
John Hattie, 7th

CONTENTS

1. The challenge 5
2. The nature of the evidence: a synthesis of meta-analyses 11
3. The argument: visible teaching and visible learning 17
4. The contributions from the student 25
5. The contributions from the home 31
6. The contributions from the school 36
7. The contributions from the teacher 43
8. The contributions from the curricula 49
9. The contributions from teaching approaches-part I 57
10. The contributions from teaching approaches-part II 64
11. Bringing it all together 74

Visit Cram101.com for full Practice Exams

Visit Cram101.com for full Practice Exams

Chapter 1. The challenge

CHAPTER OUTLINE: KEY TERMS, PEOPLE, PLACES, CONCEPTS

- Paideia
- Meta-analysis
- Explanation
- Feedback
- Reasonable doubt
- Trial
- Grammar

CHAPTER HIGHLIGHTS & NOTES: KEY TERMS, PEOPLE, PLACES, CONCEPTS

Paideia	In ancient Greek, the word n. paedeia or paideia [to educate . + - -IA suffix1] means child-rearing, education.
Meta-analysis	In statistics, a meta-analysis combines the results of several studies that address a set of related research hypotheses. In its simplest form, this is norlly by identification of a common measure of effect size, of which a weighted average might be the output of a meta-analysis. The weighting might be related to sample sizes within the individual studies.
Explanation	An explanation is a set of statements constructed to describe a set of facts which clarifies the causes, context, and consequences of those facts. This description may establish rules or laws, and may clarify the existing ones in relation to any objects, or phenomena examined. The components of an explanation can be implicit, and be interwoven with one another.
Feedback	Feedback is a process in which information about the past or the present influences the same phenomenon in the present or future. As part of a chain of cause-and-effect that forms a circuit or loop, the event is said to 'feed back' into itself.

Chapter 1. The challenge

CHAPTER HIGHLIGHTS & NOTES: KEY TERMS, PEOPLE, PLACES, CONCEPTS

	Ramaprasad (1983) defines feedback generally as 'information about the gap between the actual level and the reference level of a system parameter which is used to alter the gap in some way', and goes on to add '[t]he information on the gap between the actual level and the reference level is feedback only when it is used to alter the gap.'
	Feedback is also a synonym for:•Feedback signal - the measurement of the actual level of the parameter of interest.•Feedback loop - the complete causal path that leads from the initial detection of the gap to the subsequent modification of the gap.•Audio feedback - the howling sound that occurs when a microphone is placed too near a connected speaker, or where any loop exists between an audio input and output.•Performance appraisal - when an outside opinion or criticism is given with the intention of modifying individual or group behaviour.Overview
	Feedback is a mechanism, process or signal that is looped back to control a system within itself.
Reasonable doubt	Proof beyond a reasonable doubt is the standa of evidence required to validate a criminal conviction in most adversarial legal systems (such as the United Kingdom and the United States).
	Generally the prosecution bears the buen of proof and is required to prove their version of events to this standa. This means that the proposition being presented by the prosecution must be proven to the extent that there could be no 'reasonable doubt' in the mind of a 'reasonable person' that the defendant is guilty.
Trial	The Trial was a ship that was seized by convicts and eventually wrecked on the Mid North Coast of New South Wales, Australia in 1816.
	The Trial was a brig owned by the merchant Simeon Lord. While waiting near the Sow and Pigs Reef in Port Jackson for good winds to take it to Port Dalrymple it was seized by a group of thirteen convicts.
Grammar	In linguistics, grammar is the set of structural rules that govern the composition of clauses, phrases, and words in any given natural language. The term refers also to the study of such rules, and this field includes morphology, syntax, and phonology, often complemented by phonetics, semantics, and pragmatics. Linguists do not normally use the term to refer to orthographical rules, although usage books and style guides that call themselves grammars may also refer to spelling and punctuation.

Chapter 1. The challenge

CHAPTER QUIZ: KEY TERMS, PEOPLE, PLACES, CONCEPTS

1. In statistics, a _____ combines the results of several studies that address a set of related research hypotheses. In its simplest form, this is norlly by identification of a common measure of effect size, of which a weighted average might be the output of a _____. The weighting might be related to sample sizes within the individual studies.

    a. Motion analysis
    b. Meta-analysis
    c. Publication bias
    d. Reporting bias

2. The _____ was a ship that was seized by convicts and eventually wrecked on the Mid North Coast of New South Wales, Australia in 1816.

    The _____ was a brig owned by the merchant Simeon Lord. While waiting near the Sow and Pigs Reef in Port Jackson for good winds to take it to Port Dalrymple it was seized by a group of thirteen convicts.

    a. Barbara Harrell-Bond
    b. Trial
    c. Skeptical theism
    d. Skepticon

3. An _____ is a set of statements constructed to describe a set of facts which clarifies the causes, context, and consequences of those facts.

    This description may establish rules or laws, and may clarify the existing ones in relation to any objects, or phenomena examined. The components of an _____ can be implicit, and be interwoven with one another.

    a. Explanandum
    b. Explanation
    c. Innate intelligence
    d. Abjunction

4. In ancient Greek, the word n. paedeia or _____ [to educate . + - -IA suffix1] means child-rearing, education.

    a. Pit school
    b. Paideia
    c. Pum-Nahara Academy
    d. Pumbedita Academy

5. . _____ is a process in which information about the past or the present influences the same phenomenon in the present or future. As part of a chain of cause-and-effect that forms a circuit or loop, the event is said to 'feed back' into itself.

    Ramaprasad (1983) defines _____ generally as 'information about the gap between the actual level and the reference level of a system parameter which is used to alter the gap in some way', and goes on to add '[t]he information on the gap between the actual level and the reference level is _____ only when it is used to alter the gap.'

Chapter 1. The challenge

Visit Cram101.com for full Practice Exams

CHAPTER QUIZ: KEY TERMS, PEOPLE, PLACES, CONCEPTS

_____ is also a synonym for:•_____ signal - the measurement of the actual level of the parameter of interest.•_____ loop - the complete causal path that leads from the initial detection of the gap to the subsequent modification of the gap.•Audio _____ - the howling sound that occurs when a microphone is placed too near a connected speaker, or where any loop exists between an audio input and output.•Performance appraisal - when an outside opinion or criticism is given with the intention of modifying individual or group behaviour.Overview

_____ is a mechanism, process or signal that is looped back to control a system within itself.

a. Feedback linearization
b. Filtering problem
c. Feedback
d. First-order hold

ANSWER KEY
Chapter 1. The challenge

1. b
2. b
3. b
4. b
5. c

You can take the complete Chapter Practice Test

for Chapter 1. The challenge
on all key terms, persons, places, and concepts.

Online 99 Cents

http://www.epub207.55.20745.1.cram101.com/

Use www.Cram101.com for all your study needs

including Cram101's online interactive problem solving labs in

chemistry, statistics, mathematics, and more.

Visit Cram101.com for full Practice Exams

Chapter 2. The nature of the evidence: a synthesis of meta-analyses

CHAPTER OUTLINE: KEY TERMS, PEOPLE, PLACES, CONCEPTS

	Effect size
	Homework
	Reasonable doubt
	Feedback
	Methodology
	Mechanical work
	Barometer

CHAPTER HIGHLIGHTS & NOTES: KEY TERMS, PEOPLE, PLACES, CONCEPTS

Effect size	In statistics, an effect size is a measure of the strength of the relationship between two variabl in a statistical population, or a sample-based timate of that quantity. An effect size calculated from data is a dcriptive statistic that conveys the timated magnitude of a relationship without making any statement about whether the apparent relationship in the data reflects a true relationship in the population. In that way, effect siz complement inferential statistics such as p-valu.
Homework	Homework, refers to tasks assigned to students by their teachers to be completed outside of class. Common homework assignments may include a quantity or period of reading to be performed, writing or typing to be completed, problems to be solved, a school project to be built (such as a diorama or display), or other skills to be practiced. The basic objectives of assigning homework to students are the same as schooling in general: To increase the knowledge and improve the abilities and skills of the students.
Reasonable doubt	Proof beyond a reasonable doubt is the standa of evidence required to validate a criminal conviction in most adversarial legal systems (such as the United Kingdom and the United States).

Visit Cram101.com for full Practice Exams

Chapter 2. The nature of the evidence: a synthesis of meta-analyses

CHAPTER HIGHLIGHTS & NOTES: KEY TERMS, PEOPLE, PLACES, CONCEPTS

	Generally the prosecution bears the buen of proof and is required to prove their version of events to this standa. This means that the proposition being presented by the prosecution must be proven to the extent that there could be no 'reasonable doubt' in the mind of a 'reasonable person' that the defendant is guilty.
Feedback	Feedback is a process in which information about the past or the present influences the same phenomenon in the present or future. As part of a chain of cause-and-effect that forms a circuit or loop, the event is said to 'feed back' into itself.
	Ramaprasad (1983) defines feedback generally as 'information about the gap between the actual level and the reference level of a system parameter which is used to alter the gap in some way', and goes on to add '[t]he information on the gap between the actual level and the reference level is feedback only when it is used to alter the gap.'
	Feedback is also a synonym for:•Feedback signal - the measurement of the actual level of the parameter of interest.•Feedback loop - the complete causal path that leads from the initial detection of the gap to the subsequent modification of the gap.•Audio feedback - the howling sound that occurs when a microphone is placed too near a connected speaker, or where any loop exists between an audio input and output.•Performance appraisal - when an outside opinion or criticism is given with the intention of modifying individual or group behaviour.Overview
	Feedback is a mechanism, process or signal that is looped back to control a system within itself.
Methodology	Methodology can be:
	· 'the analysis of the principles of methods, rules, and postulates employed by a discipline'; · 'the systematic study of methods that are, can be, or have been applied within a discipline'; or · 'a particular procedure or set of procedures.'
	Methodology includes a philosophically coherent collection of theories, concepts or ideas as they relate to a particular discipline or field of inquiry:
	Methodology refers to more than a simple set of methods; rather it refers to the rationale and the philosophical assumptions that underlie a particular study relative to the scientific method. This is why scholarly literature often includes a section on the Methodology of the researchers.

Chapter 2. The nature of the evidence: a synthesis of meta-analyses

CHAPTER HIGHLIGHTS & NOTES: KEY TERMS, PEOPLE, PLACES, CONCEPTS

Mechanical work	In physics, mechanical work is the amount of energy transferred by a force acting through a distance. Like energy, it is a scalar quantity, with SI units of joules. The term work was first coined in 1826 by the French mathematician Gaspard-Gustave Coriolis.
Barometer	A Barometer is a scientific instrument used to measure atmospheric pressure. It can measure the pressure exerted by the atmosphere by using water, air, or mercury. Pressure tendency can forecast short term changes in the weather.

CHAPTER QUIZ: KEY TERMS, PEOPLE, PLACES, CONCEPTS

1. Proof beyond a _____ is the standa of evidence required to validate a criminal conviction in most adversarial legal systems (such as the United Kingdom and the United States).

    Generally the prosecution bears the buen of proof and is required to prove their version of events to this standa. This means that the proposition being presented by the prosecution must be proven to the extent that there could be no '_____' in the mind of a 'reasonable person' that the defendant is guilty.

    a. Religious skepticism
    b. Reasonable doubt
    c. Skeptical theism
    d. Skepticon

2. In statistics, an _____ is a measure of the strength of the relationship between two variabl in a statistical population, or a sample-based timate of that quantity. An _____ calculated from data is a dcriptive statistic that conveys the timated magnitude of a relationship without making any statement about whether the apparent relationship in the data reflects a true relationship in the population. In that way, effect siz complement inferential statistics such as p-valu.

    a. Inverse-variance weighting
    b. Abjunction
    c. Effect size
    d. ADD model

3. . _____ is a process in which information about the past or the present influences the same phenomenon in the present or future. As part of a chain of cause-and-effect that forms a circuit or loop, the event is said to 'feed back' into itself.

    Ramaprasad (1983) defines _____ generally as 'information about the gap between the actual level and the reference level of a system parameter which is used to alter the gap in some way', and goes on to add '[t]he information on the gap between the actual level and the reference level is _____ only when it is used to alter the gap.'

CHAPTER QUIZ: KEY TERMS, PEOPLE, PLACES, CONCEPTS

_____ is also a synonym for:•_____ signal - the measurement of the actual level of the parameter of interest.•_____ loop - the complete causal path that leads from the initial detection of the gap to the subsequent modification of the gap.•Audio _____ - the howling sound that occurs when a microphone is placed too near a connected speaker, or where any loop exists between an audio input and output.•Performance appraisal - when an outside opinion or criticism is given with the intention of modifying individual or group behaviour.Overview

_____ is a mechanism, process or signal that is looped back to control a system within itself.

  a. Feedback linearization
  b. Filtering problem
  c. Feedback
  d. First-order hold

4. _____, refers to tasks assigned to students by their teachers to be completed outside of class. Common _____ assignments may include a quantity or period of reading to be performed, writing or typing to be completed, problems to be solved, a school project to be built (such as a diorama or display), or other skills to be practiced. Main objectives and reasons for _____

The basic objectives of assigning _____ to students are the same as schooling in general: To increase the knowledge and improve the abilities and skills of the students.

  a. Human performance technology
  b. Jigsaw
  c. Homework
  d. Kinesthetic learning

5. . _____ can be:

· 'the analysis of the principles of methods, rules, and postulates employed by a discipline'; · 'the systematic study of methods that are, can be, or have been applied within a discipline'; or · 'a particular procedure or set of procedures.'

_____ includes a philosophically coherent collection of theories, concepts or ideas as they relate to a particular discipline or field of inquiry:

_____ refers to more than a simple set of methods; rather it refers to the rationale and the philosophical assumptions that underlie a particular study relative to the scientific method. This is why scholarly literature often includes a section on the _____ of the researchers. This section does more than outline the researchers' methods (as in, 'We conducted a survey of 50 people over a two-week period and subjected the results to statistical analysis', etc).; it might explain what the researchers' ontological or epistemological views are.

  a. Barbara Harrell-Bond
  b. Uniformization
  c. Methodology

Visit Cram101.com for full Practice Exams

Visit Cram101.com for full Practice Exams

ANSWER KEY
Chapter 2. The nature of the evidence: a synthesis of meta-analyses

1. b
2. c
3. c
4. c
5. c

You can take the complete Chapter Practice Test

for Chapter 2. The nature of the evidence: a synthesis of meta-analyses
on all key terms, persons, places, and concepts.

Online 99 Cents

http://www.epub207.55.20745.2.cram101.com/

Use www.Cram101.com for all your study needs

including Cram101's online interactive problem solving labs in

chemistry, statistics, mathematics, and more.

Chapter 3. The argument: visible teaching and visible learning

CHAPTER OUTLINE: KEY TERMS, PEOPLE, PLACES, CONCEPTS

- Paideia
- Learning
- Feedback
- Intention
- Facilitator
- Self-efficacy
- Coaching
- Disposition
- Engagement
- Classroom

Chapter 3. The argument: visible teaching and visible learning

CHAPTER HIGHLIGHTS & NOTES: KEY TERMS, PEOPLE, PLACES, CONCEPTS

Paideia	In ancient Greek, the word n. paedeia or paideia [to educate . + - -IA suffix1] means child-rearing, education.
Learning	Learning is acquiring new knowledge, behaviors, skills, values, preferences or understanding, and may involve synthesizing different types of information. The ability to learn is possessed by humans, animals and some machines. Progress over time tends to follow Learning curves.
Feedback	Feedback is a process in which information about the past or the present influences the same phenomenon in the present or future. As part of a chain of cause-and-effect that forms a circuit or loop, the event is said to 'feed back' into itself.
	Ramaprasad (1983) defines feedback generally as 'information about the gap between the actual level and the reference level of a system parameter which is used to alter the gap in some way', and goes on to add '[t]he information on the gap between the actual level and the reference level is feedback only when it is used to alter the gap.'
	Feedback is also a synonym for:•Feedback signal - the measurement of the actual level of the parameter of interest.•Feedback loop - the complete causal path that leads from the initial detection of the gap to the subsequent modification of the gap.•Audio feedback - the howling sound that occurs when a microphone is placed too near a connected speaker, or where any loop exists between an audio input and output.•Performance appraisal - when an outside opinion or criticism is given with the intention of modifying individual or group behaviour.Overview
	Feedback is a mechanism, process or signal that is looped back to control a system within itself.
Intention	Intention is an agent's specific purpose in performing an action or series of actions, the end or goal that is aimed at. Outcomes that are unanticipated or unforeseen are known as unintended consequences.
	Intentional behavior can also be just thoughtful and deliberate goal-directedness.
Facilitator	The term facilitation is broadly used to describe any activity which makes tasks for others easy. For example:
	· Facilitation is used in business and organisational settings to ensure the designing and running of successful meetings. · Neural facilitation in neuroscience, is the increase in postsynaptic potential evoked by a 2nd impulse. · Ecological facilitation describes how an organism profits from the presence of another. Examples are nurse plants, which provide shade for new seedlings or saplings (e.g.

Chapter 3. The argument: visible teaching and visible learning

CHAPTER HIGHLIGHTS & NOTES: KEY TERMS, PEOPLE, PLACES, CONCEPTS

using an orange tree to provide shade for a newly planted coffee plant), or plants providing shelter from wind chill in arctic environments.

A person who takes on such a role is called a facilitator. Specifically:

· A facilitator is used in a variety of group settings, including business and other organisations to describe someone whose role it is to work with group processes to ensure meetings run well and achieve a high degree of consensus. · The term facilitator is used in psychotherapy where the role is more to help group members become aware of the feelings they hold for one another · The term facilitator is used in education to refer to a specifically trained adult who sits in class with a disabled, or otherwise needy, student to help them follow the lesson that the teacher is giving · The term facilitator is used to describe people engaged in the illegal trafficking of human beings across international borders . · The term facilitator is used to describe those individuals who arrange adoptions by attempting to match available children with prospective adopters. · The term facilitator is used to describe someone who assists people with communication disorders to use communication aids with their hands.

Self-efficacy

Self-efficacy has been described as the belief that one is capable of performing in a certain manner to attain certain goals. It is a belief that one has the capabilities to execute the courses of actions required to manage prospective situations. It has been described in other ways as the concept has evolved in the literature and in society: as the sense of belief that one's actions have an effect on the environment ; as a person's judgment of his or her capabilities based on mastery criteria; a sense of a person's competence within a specific framework, focusing on the person's assessment of their abilities to perform specific tasks in relation to goals and standards rather than in comparison with others' capabilities.

Coaching

Coaching, with a professional coach, is the practice of supporting an individual, referred to as the client or mentee or coachee, through the process of achieving a specific personal or professional result.

The structures, models and methodologies of coaching are numerous but are predominantly facilitating in style; that is the coach mainly asks questions and challenges the coachee to find answers from within himself/herself based on their values, preferences and unique perspective.

Coaching is differentiated from therapeutic and counseling disciplines since clients are in most cases considered healthy (ie not sick) and move forward from their present situation.

Disposition

A disposition is a habit, a preparation, a state of readiness, or a tendency to act in a specified way.

Chapter 3. The argument: visible teaching and visible learning

CHAPTER HIGHLIGHTS & NOTES: KEY TERMS, PEOPLE, PLACES, CONCEPTS

	The terms dispositional belief and occurrent belief refer, in the former case, to a belief that is held in the mind but not currently being considered, and in the latter case, to a belief that is currently being considered by the mind.
	In Bourdieu's theory of fields dispositions are the natural tendencies of each individual to take on a certain position in any field.
Engagement	Engagement measures the extent to which a consumer has a meaningful brand experience when exposed to commercial advertising, sponsorship, television contact, or other experience.
	In March 2006 the Advertising Research Foundation defined Engagement as 'turning on a prospect to a brand idea enhanced by the surrounding context'. The ARF has also defined the function whereby engagement impacts a brand:
	Engagement is complex because a variety of exposure and relationship factors affect engagement, making simplified rankings misleading.
Classroom	A Classroom is a room in which teaching or learning activities can take place. Classrooms are found in educational institutions of all kinds, including public and private schools, corporations, and religious and humanitarian organizations. The Classroom attempts to provide a safe space where learning can take place uninterrupted by other distractions.

Chapter 3. The argument: visible teaching and visible learning

CHAPTER QUIZ: KEY TERMS, PEOPLE, PLACES, CONCEPTS

1. _____, with a professional coach, is the practice of supporting an individual, referred to as the client or mentee or coachee, through the process of achieving a specific personal or professional result.

    The structures, models and methodologies of _____ are numerous but are predominantly facilitating in style; that is the coach mainly asks questions and challenges the coachee to find answers from within himself/herself based on their values, preferences and unique perspective.

    _____ is differentiated from therapeutic and counseling disciplines since clients are in most cases considered healthy (ie not sick) and move forward from their present situation.

    a. Coaching
    b. Cognitive Assessment System
    c. Cognitive elite
    d. Cognitive load

2. _____ is a process in which information about the past or the present influences the same phenomenon in the present or future. As part of a chain of cause-and-effect that forms a circuit or loop, the event is said to 'feed back' into itself.

    Ramaprasad (1983) defines _____ generally as 'information about the gap between the actual level and the reference level of a system parameter which is used to alter the gap in some way', and goes on to add '[t]he information on the gap between the actual level and the reference level is _____ only when it is used to alter the gap.'

    _____ is also a synonym for:•_____ signal - the measurement of the actual level of the parameter of interest.•_____ loop - the complete causal path that leads from the initial detection of the gap to the subsequent modification of the gap.•Audio _____ - the howling sound that occurs when a microphone is placed too near a connected speaker, or where any loop exists between an audio input and output.•Performance appraisal - when an outside opinion or criticism is given with the intention of modifying individual or group behaviour.Overview

    _____ is a mechanism, process or signal that is looped back to control a system within itself.

    a. Feedback linearization
    b. Feedback
    c. First-order control
    d. First-order hold

3. In ancient Greek, the word n. paedeia or _____ [to educate . + - -IA suffix1] means child-rearing, education.

    a. Pit school
    b. The Price of Admission
    c. Pum-Nahara Academy
    d. Paideia

4. . _____ has been described as the belief that one is capable of performing in a certain manner to attain certain goals. It is a belief that one has the capabilities to execute the courses of actions required to manage prospective situations.

Chapter 3. The argument: visible teaching and visible learning

CHAPTER QUIZ: KEY TERMS, PEOPLE, PLACES, CONCEPTS

It has been described in other ways as the concept has evolved in the literature and in society: as the sense of belief that one's actions have an effect on the environment ; as a person's judgment of his or her capabilities based on mastery criteria; a sense of a person's competence within a specific framework, focusing on the person's assessment of their abilities to perform specific tasks in relation to goals and standards rather than in comparison with others' capabilities.

a. spirituality
b. Barbara Harrell-Bond
c. Barbinae
d. Self-efficacy

5. _____ measures the extent to which a consumer has a meaningful brand experience when exposed to commercial advertising, sponsorship, television contact, or other experience.

In March 2006 the Advertising Research Foundation defined _____ as 'turning on a prospect to a brand idea enhanced by the surrounding context'. The ARF has also defined the function whereby _____ impacts a brand:

_____ is complex because a variety of exposure and relationship factors affect _____, making simplified rankings misleading.

a. Engagement
b. Doctrine
c. Doxa
d. Doxastic logic

Visit Cram101.com for full Practice Exams

ANSWER KEY
Chapter 3. The argument: visible teaching and visible learning

1. a
2. b
3. d
4. d
5. a

You can take the complete Chapter Practice Test

for Chapter 3. The argument: visible teaching and visible learning
on all key terms, persons, places, and concepts.

Online 99 Cents

http://www.epub207.55.20745.3.cram101.com/

Use www.Cram101.com for all your study needs

including Cram101's online interactive problem solving labs in

chemistry, statistics, mathematics, and more.

Chapter 4. The contributions from the student

CHAPTER OUTLINE: KEY TERMS, PEOPLE, PLACES, CONCEPTS

	Paideia
	Disposition
	Learning
	Barometer
	Engagement
	Education
	Effect size
	Special education
	Conceptual change
	Self-efficacy
	Ethnicity
	Mechanical work

Visit Cram101.com for full Practice Exams

Chapter 4. The contributions from the student

CHAPTER HIGHLIGHTS & NOTES: KEY TERMS, PEOPLE, PLACES, CONCEPTS

Paideia	In ancient Greek, the word n. paedeia or paideia [to educate . + - -IA suffix1] means child-rearing, education.
Disposition	A disposition is a habit, a preparation, a state of readiness, or a tendency to act in a specified way. The terms dispositional belief and occurrent belief refer, in the former case, to a belief that is held in the mind but not currently being considered, and in the latter case, to a belief that is currently being considered by the mind. In Bourdieu's theory of fields dispositions are the natural tendencies of each individual to take on a certain position in any field.
Learning	Learning is acquiring new knowledge, behaviors, skills, values, preferences or understanding, and may involve synthesizing different types of information. The ability to learn is possessed by humans, animals and some machines. Progress over time tends to follow Learning curves.
Barometer	A Barometer is a scientific instrument used to measure atmospheric pressure. It can measure the pressure exerted by the atmosphere by using water, air, or mercury. Pressure tendency can forecast short term changes in the weather.
Engagement	Engagement measures the extent to which a consumer has a meaningful brand experience when exposed to commercial advertising, sponsorship, television contact, or other experience. In March 2006 the Advertising Research Foundation defined Engagement as 'turning on a prospect to a brand idea enhanced by the surrounding context'. The ARF has also defined the function whereby engagement impacts a brand: Engagement is complex because a variety of exposure and relationship factors affect engagement, making simplified rankings misleading.
Education	Education in the largest sense is any act or experience that has a formative effect on the mind, character or physical ability of an individual. In its technical sense, education is the process by which society deliberately transmits its accumulated knowledge, skills, and values from one generation to another. Etymologically, the word education is derived from educare 'bring up', which is related to educere 'bring out', 'bring forth what is within', 'bring out potential' and ducere, 'to lead'.
Effect size	In statistics, an effect size is a measure of the strength of the relationship between two variabl in a statistical population, or a sample-based timate of that quantity.

Chapter 4. The contributions from the student

CHAPTER HIGHLIGHTS & NOTES: KEY TERMS, PEOPLE, PLACES, CONCEPTS

	An effect size calculated from data is a dcriptive statistic that conveys the timated magnitude of a relationship without making any statement about whether the apparent relationship in the data reflects a true relationship in the population. In that way, effect siz complement inferential statistics such as p-valu.
Special education	Special education is the education of students with special needs in a way that address the students' individual differences and needs. Ideally, this process involves the individually planned and systematically monitored arrangement of teaching procedures, adapted equipment and materials, accessible ttings, and other interventions designed to help learners with special needs achieve a higher level of personal lf-sufficiency and success in school and community than would be available if the student were only given access to a typical classroom education.
	Common special needs include challenges with learning, communication challenges, emotional and behavioral disorders, physical disabilities, and developmental disorders.
Conceptual change	Conceptual change is the process whereby concepts and relationships between them change over the course of an individual person's lifetime or over the course of history. Research in three different fields - cognitive developmental psychology, science education, and history and philosophy of science - has sought to understand this process. Indeed, the convergence of these three fields, in their effort to understand how concepts change in content and organization, has led to the emergence of an interdisciplinary sub-field in its own right.
Self-efficacy	Self-efficacy has been described as the belief that one is capable of performing in a certain manner to attain certain goals. It is a belief that one has the capabilities to execute the courses of actions required to manage prospective situations. It has been described in other ways as the concept has evolved in the literature and in society: as the sense of belief that one's actions have an effect on the environment ; as a person's judgment of his or her capabilities based on mastery criteria; a sense of a person's competence within a specific framework, focusing on the person's assessment of their abilities to perform specific tasks in relation to goals and standards rather than in comparison with others' capabilities.
Ethnicity	Ethnicity plays a prominent role in pornography. Distinct genres of pornography focus on performers of specific ethnic groups, or on the depiction of interracial sexual activity. Ethnic pornography typically employs ethnic and racial stereotypes in its depiction of performers.
Mechanical work	In physics, mechanical work is the amount of energy transferred by a force acting through a distance. Like energy, it is a scalar quantity, with SI units of joules. The term work was first coined in 1826 by the French mathematician Gaspard-Gustave Coriolis.

Chapter 4. The contributions from the student

CHAPTER QUIZ: KEY TERMS, PEOPLE, PLACES, CONCEPTS

1. In statistics, an _____ is a measure of the strength of the relationship between two variabl in a statistical population, or a sample-based timate of that quantity. An _____ calculated from data is a dcriptive statistic that conveys the timated magnitude of a relationship without making any statement about whether the apparent relationship in the data reflects a true relationship in the population. In that way, effect siz complement inferential statistics such as p-valu.

   a. Inverse-variance weighting
   b. Emergent curriculum
   c. Effect size
   d. Adult educator

2. A _____ is a habit, a preparation, a state of readiness, or a tendency to act in a specified way.

   The terms dispositional belief and occurrent belief refer, in the former case, to a belief that is held in the mind but not currently being considered, and in the latter case, to a belief that is currently being considered by the mind.

   In Bourdieu's theory of fields _____s are the natural tendencies of each individual to take on a certain position in any field.

   a. Disquotational principle
   b. Disposition
   c. Doxa
   d. Doxastic logic

3. _____ in the largest sense is any act or experience that has a formative effect on the mind, character or physical ability of an individual. In its technical sense, _____ is the process by which society deliberately transmits its accumulated knowledge, skills, and values from one generation to another.

   Etymologically, the word _____ is derived from educare 'bring up', which is related to educere 'bring out', 'bring forth what is within', 'bring out potential' and ducere, 'to lead'.

   a. Education of the deaf
   b. Education
   c. Emergent Design
   d. Adult educator

4. _____ plays a prominent role in pornography. Distinct genres of pornography focus on performers of specific ethnic groups, or on the depiction of interracial sexual activity. Ethnic pornography typically employs ethnic and racial stereotypes in its depiction of performers.

   a. Abjunction
   b. Ethnicity
   c. Semi-continuity
   d. Semidefinite programming

5. . In ancient Greek, the word n. paedeia or _____ [to educate . + - -IA suffix1] means child-rearing, education.

a. Pit school
b. Paideia
c. Pum-Nahara Academy
d. Pumbedita Academy

ANSWER KEY
Chapter 4. The contributions from the student

1. c
2. b
3. b
4. b
5. b

You can take the complete Chapter Practice Test

for Chapter 4. The contributions from the student
on all key terms, persons, places, and concepts.

Online 99 Cents

http://www.epub207.55.20745.4.cram101.com/

Use www.Cram101.com for all your study needs

including Cram101's online interactive problem solving labs in

chemistry, statistics, mathematics, and more.

Chapter 5. The contributions from the home

CHAPTER OUTLINE: KEY TERMS, PEOPLE, PLACES, CONCEPTS

	Welfare
	Employment
	Paideia
	Homework
	Learning

CHAPTER HIGHLIGHTS & NOTES: KEY TERMS, PEOPLE, PLACES, CONCEPTS

Welfare	Welfare or Welfare work consists of actions or procedures -- especially on the part of governments and institutions -- striving to promote the basic well-being of individuals in need. These efforts usually strive to improve the financial situation of people in need but may also strive to improve their employment chances and many other aspects of their lives including sometimes their mental health. In many countries, most such aid is provided by family members, relatives, and the local community and is only theoretically available from government sources.
Employment	Employment is a contract between two parties, one being the employer and the other being the employee. An employee may be defined as: 'A person in the service of another under any contract of hire, express or implied, oral or written, where the employer has the power or right to control and direct the employee in the material details of how the work is to be performed.' Black's Law Dictionary page 471 (5th ed. 1979). In a commercial setting, the employer conceives of a productive activity, generally with the intention of generating a profit, and the employee contributes labour to the enterprise, usually in return for payment of wages.
Paideia	In ancient Greek, the word n. paedeia or paideia [to educate . + - -IA suffix1] means child-rearing, education.

Chapter 5. The contributions from the home

CHAPTER HIGHLIGHTS & NOTES: KEY TERMS, PEOPLE, PLACES, CONCEPTS

Homework	Homework, refers to tasks assigned to students by their teachers to be completed outside of class. Common homework assignments may include a quantity or period of reading to be performed, writing or typing to be completed, problems to be solved, a school project to be built (such as a diorama or display), or other skills to be practiced. The basic objectives of assigning homework to students are the same as schooling in general: To increase the knowledge and improve the abilities and skills of the students.
Learning	Learning is acquiring new knowledge, behaviors, skills, values, preferences or understanding, and may involve synthesizing different types of information. The ability to learn is possessed by humans, animals and some machines. Progress over time tends to follow Learning curves.

CHAPTER QUIZ: KEY TERMS, PEOPLE, PLACES, CONCEPTS

1. In ancient Greek, the word n. paedeia or _____ [to educate . + - -IA suffix1] means child-rearing, education.

    a. Pit school
    b. The Price of Admission
    c. Pum-Nahara Academy
    d. Paideia

2. _____ or _____ work consists of actions or procedures -- especially on the part of governments and institutions -- striving to promote the basic well-being of individuals in need. These efforts usually strive to improve the financial situation of people in need but may also strive to improve their employment chances and many other aspects of their lives including sometimes their mental health. In many countries, most such aid is provided by family members, relatives, and the local community and is only theoretically available from government sources.

    a. Barbara Harrell-Bond
    b. Barbinae
    c. Beam lead technology
    d. Welfare

3. . _____ is a contract between two parties, one being the employer and the other being the employee. An employee may be defined as: 'A person in the service of another under any contract of hire, express or implied, oral or written, where the employer has the power or right to control and direct the employee in the material details of how the work is to be performed.' Black's Law Dictionary page 471 (5th ed. 1979).

    In a commercial setting, the employer conceives of a productive activity, generally with the intention of generating a profit, and the employee contributes labour to the enterprise, usually in return for payment of wages.

Chapter 5. The contributions from the home

CHAPTER QUIZ: KEY TERMS, PEOPLE, PLACES, CONCEPTS

   a. Employment
   b. Abjunction
   c. Acoustic droplet ejection
   d. ADD model

4. _____, refers to tasks assigned to students by their teachers to be completed outside of class. Common _____ assignments may include a quantity or period of reading to be performed, writing or typing to be completed, problems to be solved, a school project to be built (such as a diorama or display), or other skills to be practiced. Main objectives and reasons for _____

   The basic objectives of assigning _____ to students are the same as schooling in general: To increase the knowledge and improve the abilities and skills of the students.

   a. Human performance technology
   b. Homework
   c. Job Shadow
   d. Kinesthetic learning

5. _____ is acquiring new knowledge, behaviors, skills, values, preferences or understanding, and may involve synthesizing different types of information. The ability to learn is possessed by humans, animals and some machines. Progress over time tends to follow _____ curves.

   a. Learning
   b. Orthodox psychotherapy
   c. United to End Racism
   d. Kinesthetic learning

ANSWER KEY
Chapter 5. The contributions from the home

1. d
2. d
3. a
4. b
5. a

You can take the complete Chapter Practice Test

for Chapter 5. The contributions from the home
on all key terms, persons, places, and concepts.

Online 99 Cents

http://www.epub207.55.20745.5.cram101.com/

Use www.Cram101.com for all your study needs

including Cram101's online interactive problem solving labs in

chemistry, statistics, mathematics, and more.

Chapter 6. The contributions from the school

CHAPTER OUTLINE: KEY TERMS, PEOPLE, PLACES, CONCEPTS

- Charter school
- Tracking
- Summer vacation
- Mobilities
- Curriculum
- Ethnicity
- Principal
- Transformational leadership
- Ability grouping
- Grammar
- Learning
- Mainstreaming
- Retention
- Acceleration
- Classroom
- Engagement
- Paideia
- School uniform

Chapter 6. The contributions from the school

CHAPTER HIGHLIGHTS & NOTES: KEY TERMS, PEOPLE, PLACES, CONCEPTS

Charter school	Charter schools are primary or secondary schools that receive public money (and like other schools, may also receive private donations) but are not subject to some of the rules, regulations, and statutes that apply to other public schools in exchange for some type of accountability for producing certain results, which are set forth in each school's charter. Charter schools are opened and attended by choice. While charter schools provide an alternative to other public schools, they are part of the public education system and are not allowed to charge tuition.
Tracking	Tracking is separating pupils by academic ability into groups for all subjects or certain classes and curriculum within a school. It may be referred as streaming or phasing in certain schools. In a tracking sysm, the entire school population is assigned to classes according to whether the students' overall achievement is above average, normal, or below average.
Summer vacation	Summer vacation (also called six weeks holiday, summer holidays (UK) or summer break) is a vacation in the summertime between school years in which students and instructors are off school typically between 6 and 12 weeks, depending on the country and district. In some countries, students participate in programs such as organized sports, summer camps, and attend summer schools. They may also hang out with friends.
Mobilities	Mobilities is a contemporary paradigm in the social sciences that explores the movement of people, ideas and things, as well as the broader social implications of those movements. A mobility 'turn' (or transformation) in the social sciences began in the 1990s in response to the increasing realization of the historic and contemporary importance of movement on individuals and society. This turn has been driven by generally increased levels of mobility and new forms of mobility where bodies combine with information and different patterns of mobility.
Curriculum	In formal education, a curriculum is the set of courses, and their content, offered at a school or university. As an idea, curriculum stems from the Latin word for race course, referring to the course of deeds and experiences through which children grow to become mature adults. A curriculum is prescriptive, and is based on a more general syllabus which merely specifies what topics must be understood and to what level to achieve a particular grade or standard.
Ethnicity	Ethnicity plays a prominent role in pornography. Distinct genres of pornography focus on performers of specific ethnic groups, or on the depiction of interracial sexual activity. Ethnic pornography typically employs ethnic and racial stereotypes in its depiction of performers.
Principal	The Principal is the chief executive and the chief academic officer of a university or college in certain parts of the Commonwealth.

Chapter 6. The contributions from the school

CHAPTER HIGHLIGHTS & NOTES: KEY TERMS, PEOPLE, PLACES, CONCEPTS

	Canada
	Queen's University and McGill University in Canada have Principals instead of Presidents, as a result of their Scottish origins. In addition the Royal Military College of Canada, and the Memorial University Campus -- Sir Wilfred Grenfell College also have principals.
Transformational leadership	Transformational leadership is defined as a leadership approach that creates valuable and positive change in the followers with the end goal of developing followers into leaders. A transformational leader focuses on 'transforming' others to help each other, to look out for each other, to be encouraging and harmonious, and to look out for the organization as a whole. With this leadership, the leader enhances the motivation, morale and performance of his followers through a variety of mechanisms.
Ability grouping	Ability grouping is the educational practice of grouping students by academic potential or past achievement.
	Ability groups are usually small, informal groups formed within a single classroom. Assignment to an ability group is often short-term (never lasting longer than one school year), and varies by subject (Gamoran 1992).
Grammar	In linguistics, grammar is the set of structural rules that govern the composition of clauses, phrases, and words in any given natural language. The term refers also to the study of such rules, and this field includes morphology, syntax, and phonology, often complemented by phonetics, semantics, and pragmatics. Linguists do not normally use the term to refer to orthographical rules, although usage books and style guides that call themselves grammars may also refer to spelling and punctuation.
Learning	Learning is acquiring new knowledge, behaviors, skills, values, preferences or understanding, and may involve synthesizing different types of information. The ability to learn is possessed by humans, animals and some machines. Progress over time tends to follow Learning curves.
Mainstreaming	Pilot or policy Mainstreaming is the act of broadening the application of a change or innovation from a small-scale pilot to the whole of a programme or policy domain. It involves recognising that the results of an experiment are positive and the learning deserves to be applied more widely. It thus requires three mechanisms, to:•finance and conduct experiments•distinguish success from failure•scale up the successes
	Other related terms include capacity building and embedding.
Retention	Retention can have the following meanings:

Chapter 6. The contributions from the school

CHAPTER HIGHLIGHTS & NOTES: KEY TERMS, PEOPLE, PLACES, CONCEPTS

	· Retention basin, instance retaining (e.g. water in the ground) · In learning: it is the ability to retain facts and figures in memory (spaced repetition) · Grade Retention, in schools, keeping a student in the same grade for another year (that is, not promoting the student to the next higher grade with his/her classmates) · Retention period, in Usenet, the time a news server holds a newsgroup posting before deleting it as no longer relevant · Judicial Retention, in the United States court system, a process whereby a judge is periodically subject to a vote in order to remain in the position of judge · Urinary Retention, the lack or inability to urinate · Employee Retention, the ability to keep employees within an organization · Retention agent is a process chemical
Acceleration	In physics, and more specifically kinematics, Acceleration is the change in velocity over time. Because velocity is a vector, it can change in two ways: a change in magnitude and/or a change in direction. In one dimension, i.e.
Classroom	A Classroom is a room in which teaching or learning activities can take place. Classrooms are found in educational institutions of all kinds, including public and private schools, corporations, and religious and humanitarian organizations. The Classroom attempts to provide a safe space where learning can take place uninterrupted by other distractions.
Engagement	Engagement measures the extent to which a consumer has a meaningful brand experience when exposed to commercial advertising, sponsorship, television contact, or other experience. In March 2006 the Advertising Research Foundation defined Engagement as 'turning on a prospect to a brand idea enhanced by the surrounding context'. The ARF has also defined the function whereby engagement impacts a brand: Engagement is complex because a variety of exposure and relationship factors affect engagement, making simplified rankings misleading.
Paideia	In ancient Greek, the word n. paedeia or paideia [to educate . + - -IA suffix1] means child-rearing, education.
School uniform	A school uniform is an outfit--a set of standardized clothes--worn primarily for an educational institution. They are common in primary and secondary schools in various countries . When used, they form the basis of a school's dress code.

Chapter 6. The contributions from the school

CHAPTER QUIZ: KEY TERMS, PEOPLE, PLACES, CONCEPTS

1. The _____ is the chief executive and the chief academic officer of a university or college in certain parts of the Commonwealth.

    Canada

    Queen's University and McGill University in Canada have _____s instead of Presidents, as a result of their Scottish origins. In addition the Royal Military College of Canada, and the Memorial University Campus -- Sir Wilfred Grenfell College also have _____s.

    a. Barbara Harrell-Bond
    b. Principal
    c. Behavioral cusp
    d. BHI horology course

2. In linguistics, _____ is the set of structural rules that govern the composition of clauses, phrases, and words in any given natural language. The term refers also to the study of such rules, and this field includes morphology, syntax, and phonology, often complemented by phonetics, semantics, and pragmatics. Linguists do not normally use the term to refer to orthographical rules, although usage books and style guides that call themselves _____s may also refer to spelling and punctuation.

    a. Task
    b. Grammar
    c. Risk assessment
    d. Scale of one to ten

3. In formal education, a _____ is the set of courses, and their content, offered at a school or university. As an idea, _____ stems from the Latin word for race course, referring to the course of deeds and experiences through which children grow to become mature adults. A _____ is prescriptive, and is based on a more general syllabus which merely specifies what topics must be understood and to what level to achieve a particular grade or standard.

    a. Transfer credit
    b. Course catalog
    c. Behavioral cusp
    d. Curriculum

4. Tracking is separating pupils by academic ability into groups for all subjects or certain classes and curriculum within a school. It may be referred as streaming or phasing in certain schools. In a _____ sysm, the entire school population is assigned to classes according to whether the students' overall achievement is above average, normal, or below average.

    a. Tracking
    b. Woburn Collegiate Institute
    c. The Woodlands School
    d. Country Day School movement

Chapter 6. The contributions from the school

CHAPTER QUIZ: KEY TERMS, PEOPLE, PLACES, CONCEPTS

5. _____ is the educational practice of grouping students by academic potential or past achievement.

Ability groups are usually small, informal groups formed within a single classroom. Assignment to an ability group is often short-term (never lasting longer than one school year), and varies by subject (Gamoran 1992).

a. Acting white
b. Ability grouping
c. Education 3.0
d. End of Course Test

ANSWER KEY
Chapter 6. The contributions from the school

1. b
2. b
3. d
4. a
5. b

You can take the complete Chapter Practice Test

for Chapter 6. The contributions from the school
on all key terms, persons, places, and concepts.

Online 99 Cents

http://www.epub207.55.20745.6.cram101.com/

Use www.Cram101.com for all your study needs

including Cram101's online interactive problem solving labs in

chemistry, statistics, mathematics, and more.

Chapter 7. The contributions from the teacher

CHAPTER OUTLINE: KEY TERMS, PEOPLE, PLACES, CONCEPTS

	Mechanical work
	Paideia
	Intention
	Learning
	Classroom
	Ethnicity
	Engagement
	Professional development

CHAPTER HIGHLIGHTS & NOTES: KEY TERMS, PEOPLE, PLACES, CONCEPTS

Mechanical work	In physics, mechanical work is the amount of energy transferred by a force acting through a distance. Like energy, it is a scalar quantity, with SI units of joules. The term work was first coined in 1826 by the French mathematician Gaspard-Gustave Coriolis.
Paideia	In ancient Greek, the word n. paedeia or paideia [to educate . + - -IA suffix1] means child-rearing, education.
Intention	Intention is an agent's specific purpose in performing an action or series of actions, the end or goal that is aimed at. Outcomes that are unanticipated or unforeseen are known as unintended consequences. Intentional behavior can also be just thoughtful and deliberate goal-directedness.
Learning	Learning is acquiring new knowledge, behaviors, skills, values, preferences or understanding, and may involve synthesizing different types of information. The ability to learn is possessed by humans, animals and some machines.

Visit Cram101.com for full Practice Exams

Chapter 7. The contributions from the teacher

CHAPTER HIGHLIGHTS & NOTES: KEY TERMS, PEOPLE, PLACES, CONCEPTS

Classroom	A Classroom is a room in which teaching or learning activities can take place. Classrooms are found in educational institutions of all kinds, including public and private schools, corporations, and religious and humanitarian organizations. The Classroom attempts to provide a safe space where learning can take place uninterrupted by other distractions.
Ethnicity	Ethnicity plays a prominent role in pornography. Distinct genres of pornography focus on performers of specific ethnic groups, or on the depiction of interracial sexual activity. Ethnic pornography typically employs ethnic and racial stereotypes in its depiction of performers.
Engagement	Engagement measures the extent to which a consumer has a meaningful brand experience when exposed to commercial advertising, sponsorship, television contact, or other experience. In March 2006 the Advertising Research Foundation defined Engagement as 'turning on a prospect to a brand idea enhanced by the surrounding context'. The ARF has also defined the function whereby engagement impacts a brand: Engagement is complex because a variety of exposure and relationship factors affect engagement, making simplified rankings misleading.
Professional development	Professional development refers to skills and knowledge attained for both personal development and career advancement. Professional development encompasses all types of facilitated learning opportunities, ranging from college degrees to formal coursework, conferences and informal learning opportunities situated in practice. It has been described as intensive and collaborative, ideally incorporating an evaluative stage There are a variety of approaches to professional development, including consultation, coaching, communities of practice, lesson study, mentoring, reflective supervision and technical assistance.

Chapter 7. The contributions from the teacher

CHAPTER QUIZ: KEY TERMS, PEOPLE, PLACES, CONCEPTS

1. _____ measures the extent to which a consumer has a meaningful brand experience when exposed to commercial advertising, sponsorship, television contact, or other experience.

    In March 2006 the Advertising Research Foundation defined _____ as 'turning on a prospect to a brand idea enhanced by the surrounding context'. The ARF has also defined the function whereby _____ impacts a brand:

    _____ is complex because a variety of exposure and relationship factors affect _____, making simplified rankings misleading.

    a. Abjunction
    b. Recognition
    c. Risk assessment
    d. Engagement

2. _____ is an agent's specific purpose in performing an action or series of actions, the end or goal that is aimed at. Outcomes that are unanticipated or unforeseen are known as unintended consequences.

    Intentional behavior can also be just thoughtful and deliberate goal-directedness.

    a. Intuition
    b. Intention
    c. Cyclotomic polynomial
    d. Cylindrical algebraic decomposition

3. In physics, _____ is the amount of energy transferred by a force acting through a distance. Like energy, it is a scalar quantity, with SI units of joules. The term work was first coined in 1826 by the French mathematician Gaspard-Gustave Coriolis.

    a. Relative humidity
    b. Solubility
    c. Heat capacity
    d. Mechanical work

4. _____ refers to skills and knowledge attained for both personal development and career advancement. _____ encompasses all types of facilitated learning opportunities, ranging from college degrees to formal coursework, conferences and informal learning opportunities situated in practice. It has been described as intensive and collaborative, ideally incorporating an evaluative stage There are a variety of approaches to _____, including consultation, coaching, communities of practice, lesson study, mentoring, reflective supervision and technical assistance.

    a. Professional development
    b. Renton Technical College
    c. Ringsend Technical Institute
    d. St. Clair County Technical Education Center

5. . In ancient Greek, the word n. paedeia or _____ [to educate . + - -IA suffix1] means child-rearing, education.

a. Pit school
b. The Price of Admission
c. Paideia
d. Pumbedita Academy

ANSWER KEY
Chapter 7. The contributions from the teacher

1. d
2. b
3. d
4. a
5. c

You can take the complete Chapter Practice Test

for Chapter 7. The contributions from the teacher
on all key terms, persons, places, and concepts.

Online 99 Cents

http://www.epub207.55.20745.7.cram101.com/

Use www.Cram101.com for all your study needs

including Cram101's online interactive problem solving labs in

chemistry, statistics, mathematics, and more.

Chapter 8. The contributions from the curricula

CHAPTER OUTLINE: KEY TERMS, PEOPLE, PLACES, CONCEPTS

- National Reading Panel
- Learning
- Perception
- Visual perception
- Vocabulary
- Phonics
- Paideia
- Phonemic awareness
- Direct instruction
- Whole language
- Reading Recovery
- Fourth grade
- Feedback
- Coaching
- Education
- Social skills
- Values
- Acceleration
- Intention

Visit Cram101.com for full Practice Exams

Chapter 8. The contributions from the curricula

CHAPTER HIGHLIGHTS & NOTES: KEY TERMS, PEOPLE, PLACES, CONCEPTS

National Reading Panel	The National Reading Panel was a United States government body. Formed in 1997 at the request of Congress, it was a national panel with the stated aim of assessing the effectiveness of different approaches used to teach children to read. The panel was created by Director of the National Institute of Child Health and Human Development (NICHD) at the National Institutes of Health, in consultation with the Secretary of Education, and included prominent experts in the fields of reading education, psychology, and higher education.
Learning	Learning is acquiring new knowledge, behaviors, skills, values, preferences or understanding, and may involve synthesizing different types of information. The ability to learn is possessed by humans, animals and some machines. Progress over time tends to follow Learning curves.
Perception	Perception is the process of attaining awareness or understanding of the environment by organizing and interpreting sensory information. All perception involves signals in the nervous system, which in turn result from physical stimulation of the sense organs. For example, vision involves light striking the retinas of the eyes, smell is mediated by odor molecules and hearing involves pressure waves.
Visual perception	Visual perception is the ability to interpret information and surroundings from the effects of visible light reaching the eye. The resulting perception is also known as eyesight, sight, or vision (adjectival form: visual, optical, or ocular). The various physiological components involved in vision are referred to collectively as the visual system, and are the focus of much research in psychology, cognitive science, neuroscience, and molecular biology.
Vocabulary	A person's vocabulary is the set of words within a language that are familiar to that person. A vocabulary usually develops with age, and serves as a useful and fundamental tool for communication and acquiring knowledge. Acquiring an extensive vocabulary is one of the largest challenges in learning a second language.
Phonics	Phonics is a method for teaching reading and writing by developing learners' phonemic awareness--the ability to hear, identify, and manipulate English phonemes-- in order to teach the correspondence between these sounds and the spelling patterns (graphemes) that represent them. The goal of phonics is to enable beginning readers to decode new written words by sounding them out, or in phonics terms, blending the sound-spelling patterns. Since it focuses on the spoken and written units within words, phonics is a sublexical approach and, as a result, is often contrasted with Whole language, a word-level-up philosophy for teaching reading.
Paideia	In ancient Greek, the word n. paedeia or paideia [to educate .

Chapter 8. The contributions from the curricula

CHAPTER HIGHLIGHTS & NOTES: KEY TERMS, PEOPLE, PLACES, CONCEPTS

Phonemic awareness	Phonemic awareness is a subset of phonological awareness in which listeners are able to hear, identify and manipulate phonemes, the smallest units of sound that can differentiate meaning. Serating the spoken word 'cat' into three distinct phonemes, /k/, /æ/, and /t/, requires phonemic awareness. The National Reading nel has found that phonemic awareness improves children's word reading and reading comprehension, as well as helping children learn to spell.
Direct instruction	Direct instruction is a general term for the explicit teaching of a skill-set using lectures or demonstrations of the material, rather than exploratory models such as inquiry-based learning. This method is often contrasted with tutorials, participatory laboratory classes, discussion, recitation, seminars, workshops, observation, case study, active learning, practica or internships. Usually it involves explication of the skill or subject matter to be taught and may or may not include an opportunity for student participation or individual practice.
Whole language	Whole language describes a literacy philosophy which emphasizes that children should focus on meaning and strategy instruction. It is often contrasted with phonics-based methods of teaching reading and writing which emphasize instruction for decoding and spelling. However, from whole language practitioners' perspective this view is erroneous and sets up a false dichotomy.
Reading Recovery	Reading Recovery is a school-based, short-term intervention designed for children aged five or six, who are the lowest literacy achievers after their first year of school. These children are often not able to read the simplest of books or even write their own name before the intervention. The intervention involves intensive one-to-one lessons for 30 minutes a day with a trained literacy teacher, for an average of 20 weeks.
Fourth grade	Fourth grade is a year of education in the United States and many other nations. The fourth grade is the fourth school year after kindergarten. Students are usually 9 or 10 years old, depending on their birthday.
Feedback	Feedback is a process in which information about the past or the present influences the same phenomenon in the present or future. As part of a chain of cause-and-effect that forms a circuit or loop, the event is said to 'feed back' into itself. Ramaprasad (1983) defines feedback generally as 'information about the gap between the actual level and the reference level of a system parameter which is used to alter the gap in some way', and goes on to add '[t]he information on the gap between the actual level and the reference level is feedback only when it is used to alter the gap.'

Chapter 8. The contributions from the curricula

CHAPTER HIGHLIGHTS & NOTES: KEY TERMS, PEOPLE, PLACES, CONCEPTS

	Feedback is also a synonym for:•Feedback signal - the measurement of the actual level of the parameter of interest.•Feedback loop - the complete causal path that leads from the initial detection of the gap to the subsequent modification of the gap.•Audio feedback - the howling sound that occurs when a microphone is placed too near a connected speaker, or where any loop exists between an audio input and output.•Performance appraisal - when an outside opinion or criticism is given with the intention of modifying individual or group behaviour.Overview
	Feedback is a mechanism, process or signal that is looped back to control a system within itself.
Coaching	Coaching, with a professional coach, is the practice of supporting an individual, referred to as the client or mentee or coachee, through the process of achieving a specific personal or professional result.
	The structures, models and methodologies of coaching are numerous but are predominantly facilitating in style; that is the coach mainly asks questions and challenges the coachee to find answers from within himself/herself based on their values, preferences and unique perspective.
	Coaching is differentiated from therapeutic and counseling disciplines since clients are in most cases considered healthy (ie not sick) and move forward from their present situation.
Education	Education in the largest sense is any act or experience that has a formative effect on the mind, character or physical ability of an individual. In its technical sense, education is the process by which society deliberately transmits its accumulated knowledge, skills, and values from one generation to another.
	Etymologically, the word education is derived from educare 'bring up', which is related to educere 'bring out', 'bring forth what is within', 'bring out potential' and ducere, 'to lead'.
Social skills	In behaviourism, social skill is any skill facilitating interaction and communication with others. Social rules and relations are created, communicated, and changed in verbal and nonverbal ways. The process of learning such skills is called socialization. The rationale for this type of an approach to treatment is that people meet a variety of social problems and can reduce the stress and punishment from the encounter as well as increase their reinforcement by having the correct skills.

Chapter 8. The contributions from the curricula

CHAPTER HIGHLIGHTS & NOTES: KEY TERMS, PEOPLE, PLACES, CONCEPTS

Values	The values embodied in cultural heritage are identified in order to assess significance, prioritize resources, and inform conservation decision-making. It is recognised that values may compete and change over time, and that heritage may have different meanings for different stakeholders. Alois Riegl is credited with developing Ruskin's concept of 'voicefulness' into a systematic categorization of the different values of a monument.
Acceleration	In physics, and more specifically kinematics, Acceleration is the change in velocity over time. Because velocity is a vector, it can change in two ways: a change in magnitude and/or a change in direction. In one dimension, i.e.
Intention	Intention is an agent's specific purpose in performing an action or series of actions, the end or goal that is aimed at. Outcomes that are unanticipated or unforeseen are known as unintended consequences. Intentional behavior can also be just thoughtful and deliberate goal-directedness.

CHAPTER QUIZ: KEY TERMS, PEOPLE, PLACES, CONCEPTS

1. _____ is the ability to interpret information and surroundings from the effects of visible light reaching the eye. The resulting perception is also known as eyesight, sight, or vision (adjectival form: visual, optical, or ocular). The various physiological components involved in vision are referred to collectively as the visual system, and are the focus of much research in psychology, cognitive science, neuroscience, and molecular biology.

    a. Visual space
    b. Reconstructive observation
    c. Testimony
    d. Visual perception

2. _____ describes a literacy philosophy which emphasizes that children should focus on meaning and strategy instruction. It is often contrasted with phonics-based methods of teaching reading and writing which emphasize instruction for decoding and spelling. However, from _____ practitioners' perspective this view is erroneous and sets up a false dichotomy.

    a. Worked-example effect
    b. Divergent question
    c. Whole language
    d. Dual-coding theory

3. . The _____ was a United States government body. Formed in 1997 at the request of Congress, it was a national panel with the stated aim of assessing the effectiveness of different approaches used to teach children to read.

CHAPTER QUIZ: KEY TERMS, PEOPLE, PLACES, CONCEPTS

The panel was created by Director of the National Institute of Child Health and Human Development (NICHD) at the National Institutes of Health, in consultation with the Secretary of Education, and included prominent experts in the fields of reading education, psychology, and higher education.

- a. Center for Applied Special Technology
- b. National Reading Panel
- c. Barbinae
- d. Beam lead technology

4. _____ is acquiring new knowledge, behaviors, skills, values, preferences or understanding, and may involve synthesizing different types of information. The ability to learn is possessed by humans, animals and some machines. Progress over time tends to follow _____ curves.

- a. Barbara Harrell-Bond
- b. Barbinae
- c. Learning
- d. Being-in-itself

5. _____ is the process of attaining awareness or understanding of the environment by organizing and interpreting sensory information. All _____ involves signals in the nervous system, which in turn result from physical stimulation of the sense organs. For example, vision involves light striking the retinas of the eyes, smell is mediated by odor molecules and hearing involves pressure waves.

- a. Perceptual learning
- b. Perception
- c. Testimony
- d. Thought experiment

ANSWER KEY
Chapter 8. The contributions from the curricula

1. d
2. c
3. b
4. c
5. b

You can take the complete Chapter Practice Test

for Chapter 8. The contributions from the curricula
on all key terms, persons, places, and concepts.

Online 99 Cents

http://www.epub207.55.20745.8.cram101.com/

Use www.Cram101.com for all your study needs

including Cram101's online interactive problem solving labs in

chemistry, statistics, mathematics, and more.

Visit Cram101.com for full Practice Exams

Chapter 9. The contributions from teaching approaches-part I

CHAPTER OUTLINE: KEY TERMS, PEOPLE, PLACES, CONCEPTS

- Intention
- Learning
- Education
- Special education
- Paideia
- Self-efficacy
- Concepts
- Coaching
- Mastery learning
- Feedback
- Formative evaluation
- Study skills
- Learning styles

Chapter 9. The contributions from teaching approaches-part I

CHAPTER HIGHLIGHTS & NOTES: KEY TERMS, PEOPLE, PLACES, CONCEPTS

Intention	Intention is an agent's specific purpose in performing an action or series of actions, the end or goal that is aimed at. Outcomes that are unanticipated or unforeseen are known as unintended consequences. Intentional behavior can also be just thoughtful and deliberate goal-directedness.
Learning	Learning is acquiring new knowledge, behaviors, skills, values, preferences or understanding, and may involve synthesizing different types of information. The ability to learn is possessed by humans, animals and some machines. Progress over time tends to follow Learning curves.
Education	Education in the largest sense is any act or experience that has a formative effect on the mind, character or physical ability of an individual. In its technical sense, education is the process by which society deliberately transmits its accumulated knowledge, skills, and values from one generation to another. Etymologically, the word education is derived from educare 'bring up', which is related to educere 'bring out', 'bring forth what is within', 'bring out potential' and ducere, 'to lead'.
Special education	Special education is the education of students with special needs in a way that address the students' individual differences and needs. Ideally, this process involves the individually planned and systematically monitored arrangement of teaching procedures, adapted equipment and materials, accessible ttings, and other interventions designed to help learners with special needs achieve a higher level of personal lf-sufficiency and success in school and community than would be available if the student were only given access to a typical classroom education. Common special needs include challenges with learning, communication challenges, emotional and behavioral disorders, physical disabilities, and developmental disorders.
Paideia	In ancient Greek, the word n. paedeia or paideia [to educate . + - -IA suffix1] means child-rearing, education.
Self-efficacy	Self-efficacy has been described as the belief that one is capable of performing in a certain manner to attain certain goals. It is a belief that one has the capabilities to execute the courses of actions required to manage prospective situations. It has been described in other ways as the concept has evolved in the literature and in society: as the sense of belief that one's actions have an effect on the environment ; as a person's judgment of his or her capabilities based on mastery criteria; a sense of a person's competence within a specific framework, focusing on the person's assessment of their abilities to perform specific tasks in relation to goals and standards rather than in comparison with others' capabilities.

Chapter 9. The contributions from teaching approaches-part I

CHAPTER HIGHLIGHTS & NOTES: KEY TERMS, PEOPLE, PLACES, CONCEPTS

Concepts	There are two prevailing theories in contemporary philosophy which attempt to explain the nature of Concepts. The representational theory of mind proposes that Concepts are mental representations, while the semantic theory of Concepts holds that they are abstract objects. Ideas are taken to be Concepts, although abstract Concepts do not necessarily appear to the mind as images as some ideas do.
Coaching	Coaching, with a professional coach, is the practice of supporting an individual, referred to as the client or mentee or coachee, through the process of achieving a specific personal or professional result. The structures, models and methodologies of coaching are numerous but are predominantly facilitating in style; that is the coach mainly asks questions and challenges the coachee to find answers from within himself/herself based on their values, preferences and unique perspective. Coaching is differentiated from therapeutic and counseling disciplines since clients are in most cases considered healthy (ie not sick) and move forward from their present situation.
Mastery learning	In Mastery learning, 'the students are helped to master each learning unit before proceeding to a more advanced learning task' (Bloom 1985) in contrast to 'conventional instruction'. Thus, the students are not advanced to a subsequent learning objective until they demonstrate proficiency with the current one. Mastery learning curricula generally consist of discrete topics which all students begin together.
Feedback	Feedback is a process in which information about the past or the present influences the same phenomenon in the present or future. As part of a chain of cause-and-effect that forms a circuit or loop, the event is said to 'feed back' into itself. Ramaprasad (1983) defines feedback generally as 'information about the gap between the actual level and the reference level of a system parameter which is used to alter the gap in some way', and goes on to add '[t]he information on the gap between the actual level and the reference level is feedback only when it is used to alter the gap.' Feedback is also a synonym for:•Feedback signal - the measurement of the actual level of the parameter of interest.•Feedback loop - the complete causal path that leads from the initial detection of the gap to the subsequent modification of the gap.•Audio feedback - the howling sound that occurs when a microphone is placed too near a connected speaker, or where any loop exists between an audio input and output.•Performance appraisal - when an outside opinion or criticism is given with the intention of modifying individual or group behaviour.Overview

Chapter 9. The contributions from teaching approaches-part I

CHAPTER HIGHLIGHTS & NOTES: KEY TERMS, PEOPLE, PLACES, CONCEPTS

Formative evaluation	Formative evaluation is a type of evaluation which has the purpose of improving programs. It goes under other names such as developmental evaluation and implementation evaluation. It can be contrasted with other types of evaluation which have other purposes, in particular process evaluation and outcome evaluation.
Study skills	Study skills are approaches applied to learning. They are generally critical to succe in school, are considered eential for acquiring good grades, and are useful for learning throughout one's life. There are an array of study skills, which may tackle the proce of organising and taking in new information, retaining information, or dealing with aements.
Learning styles	Learning styles are various approaches or ways of learning. They involve educating methods, particular to an individual, that are presumed to allow that individual to learn best. Most people prefer an identifiable method of interacting with, taking in, and processing stimuli or information.

CHAPTER QUIZ: KEY TERMS, PEOPLE, PLACES, CONCEPTS

1. _____ has been described as the belief that one is capable of performing in a certain manner to attain certain goals. It is a belief that one has the capabilities to execute the courses of actions required to manage prospective situations. It has been described in other ways as the concept has evolved in the literature and in society: as the sense of belief that one's actions have an effect on the environment ; as a person's judgment of his or her capabilities based on mastery criteria; a sense of a person's competence within a specific framework, focusing on the person's assessment of their abilities to perform specific tasks in relation to goals and standards rather than in comparison with others' capabilities.

    a. Self-efficacy
    b. Barbara Harrell-Bond
    c. Barbinae
    d. Music jury

2. _____ is an agent's specific purpose in performing an action or series of actions, the end or goal that is aimed at. Outcomes that are unanticipated or unforeseen are known as unintended consequences.

    Intentional behavior can also be just thoughtful and deliberate goal-directedness.

    a. Intuition
    b. Unconscious mind
    c. Abjunction
    d. Intention

3. . There are two prevailing theories in contemporary philosophy which attempt to explain the nature of _____.

Chapter 9. The contributions from teaching approaches-part I

CHAPTER QUIZ: KEY TERMS, PEOPLE, PLACES, CONCEPTS

The representational theory of mind proposes that _____ are mental representations, while the semantic theory of _____ holds that they are abstract objects. Ideas are taken to be _____, although abstract _____ do not necessarily appear to the mind as images as some ideas do.

- a. Cratylism
- b. Concepts
- c. Pragmatics
- d. Sign

4. _____, with a professional coach, is the practice of supporting an individual, referred to as the client or mentee or coachee, through the process of achieving a specific personal or professional result.

The structures, models and methodologies of _____ are numerous but are predominantly facilitating in style; that is the coach mainly asks questions and challenges the coachee to find answers from within himself/herself based on their values, preferences and unique perspective.

_____ is differentiated from therapeutic and counseling disciplines since clients are in most cases considered healthy (ie not sick) and move forward from their present situation.

- a. Cognitive apprenticeship
- b. Cognitive Assessment System
- c. Coaching
- d. Cognitive load

5. _____ is the education of students with special needs in a way that address the students' individual differences and needs. Ideally, this process involves the individually planned and systematically monitored arrangement of teaching procedures, adapted equipment and materials, accessible ttings, and other interventions designed to help learners with special needs achieve a higher level of personal lf-sufficiency and success in school and community than would be available if the student were only given access to a typical classroom education.

Common special needs include challenges with learning, communication challenges, emotional and behavioral disorders, physical disabilities, and developmental disorders.

- a. STARBASE
- b. Special education
- c. Summer Discovery
- d. Super 30

Visit Cram101.com for full Practice Exams

ANSWER KEY
Chapter 9. The contributions from teaching approaches-part I

1. a
2. d
3. b
4. c
5. b

You can take the complete Chapter Practice Test

for Chapter 9. The contributions from teaching approaches-part I

on all key terms, persons, places, and concepts.

Online 99 Cents

http://www.epub207.55.20745.9.cram101.com/

Use www.Cram101.com for all your study needs

including Cram101's online interactive problem solving labs in

chemistry, statistics, mathematics, and more.

Chapter 10. The contributions from teaching approaches-part II

CHAPTER OUTLINE: KEY TERMS, PEOPLE, PLACES, CONCEPTS

	Reciprocal teaching
	Direct instruction
	Engagement
	Intention
	Learning
	Project Follow Through
	Acceleration
	Education
	Special education
	Problem solving
	Problem-based learning
	Competitive learning
	Cooperative learning
	Paideia
	TEAMS
	Effect size
	Grammar
	Mastery learning
	Feedback

Visit Cram101.com for full Practice Exams

Chapter 10. The contributions from teaching approaches-part II

CHAPTER OUTLINE: KEY TERMS, PEOPLE, PLACES, CONCEPTS

- Multimedia learning
- Programmed instruction
- Distance education
- Out-of-school learning
- Homework
- Coaching

CHAPTER HIGHLIGHTS & NOTES: KEY TERMS, PEOPLE, PLACES, CONCEPTS

Reciprocal teaching	Reciprocal teaching is an instructional activity that takes the form of a dialogue between teachers and students regarding segments of text. Reciprocal teaching is a reading technique which is thought to promote the teaching process. A reciprocal approach provides students with four specific reading strategies that are actively and consciously used as texts - Questioning, Clarifying, Summarizing, and Predicting.
Direct instruction	Direct instruction is a general term for the explicit teaching of a skill-set using lectures or demonstrations of the material, rather than exploratory models such as inquiry-based learning. This method is often contrasted with tutorials, participatory laboratory classes, discussion, recitation, seminars, workshops, observation, case study, active learning, practica or internships. Usually it involves explication of the skill or subject matter to be taught and may or may not include an opportunity for student participation or individual practice.
Engagement	Engagement measures the extent to which a consumer has a meaningful brand experience when exposed to commercial advertising, sponsorship, television contact, or other experience. In March 2006 the Advertising Research Foundation defined Engagement as 'turning on a prospect to a brand idea enhanced by the surrounding context'. The ARF has also defined the function whereby engagement impacts a brand:

Chapter 10. The contributions from teaching approaches-part II

CHAPTER HIGHLIGHTS & NOTES: KEY TERMS, PEOPLE, PLACES, CONCEPTS

Intention	Intention is an agent's specific purpose in performing an action or series of actions, the end or goal that is aimed at. Outcomes that are unanticipated or unforeseen are known as unintended consequences. Intentional behavior can also be just thoughtful and deliberate goal-directedness.
Learning	Learning is acquiring new knowledge, behaviors, skills, values, preferences or understanding, and may involve synthesizing different types of information. The ability to learn is possessed by humans, animals and some machines. Progress over time tends to follow Learning curves.
Project Follow Through	Project Follow Through was the largest and most expensive experiment in education funded by the U.S. federal government that has ever been conducted. The most extensive evaluation of Follow Through data covers the years 1968-1977; however, the program continued to receive funding from the government until 1995 (Egbert, 1981, p. 7). Follow Through was originally intended to be an extension of the federal Head Start program, which delivered educational, health, and social services to typically disadvantaged preschool children and their families.
Acceleration	In physics, and more specifically kinematics, Acceleration is the change in velocity over time. Because velocity is a vector, it can change in two ways: a change in magnitude and/or a change in direction. In one dimension, i.e.
Education	Education in the largest sense is any act or experience that has a formative effect on the mind, character or physical ability of an individual. In its technical sense, education is the process by which society deliberately transmits its accumulated knowledge, skills, and values from one generation to another. Etymologically, the word education is derived from educare 'bring up', which is related to educere 'bring out', 'bring forth what is within', 'bring out potential' and ducere, 'to lead'.
Special education	Special education is the education of students with special needs in a way that address the students' individual differences and needs. Ideally, this process involves the individually planned and systematically monitored arrangement of teaching procedures, adapted equipment and materials, accessible ttings, and other interventions designed to help learners with special needs achieve a higher level of personal lf-sufficiency and success in school and community than would be available if the student were only given access to a typical classroom education. Common special needs include challenges with learning, communication challenges, emotional and behavioral disorders, physical disabilities, and developmental disorders.
Problem solving	Problem solving is a mental process and is part of the larger problem process that includes problem finding and problem shaping.

Chapter 10. The contributions from teaching approaches-part II

CHAPTER HIGHLIGHTS & NOTES: KEY TERMS, PEOPLE, PLACES, CONCEPTS

	Considered the most complex of all intellectual functions, problem solving has been defined as higher-order cognitive process that requires the modulation and control of more routine or fundamental skills. Problem solving occurs when an organism or an artificial intelligence system needs to move from a given state to a desired goal state.
Problem-based learning	Problem-based learning is a student-centered pedagogy in which students learn about a subject in the context of comex, multifaceted, and realistic problems (not to be confused with project-based learning). The goals of are to help the students develop flexible knowledge, effective problem solving skills, self-directed learning, effective collaboration skills and intrinsic motivation. Working in groups, students identify what they already know, what they need to know, and how and where to access new information that may lead to resolution of the problem.
Competitive learning	Competitive learning is a form of unsupervised learning in artificial neural networks, in which nodes compete for the right to respond to a subset of the input data. A variant of Hebbian learning, competitive learning works by increasing the specialization of each node in the network. It is well suited to finding usters within data.
Cooperative learning	Cooperative learning is an approach to organizing assroom activities into academic and social learning experiences. It differs from group work, and it has been described as 'structuring positive interdependence.' Students must work in groups to complete tasks collectively toward academic goals. Unlike individual learning, which can be competitive in nature, students learning cooperatively capitalize on one another's resources and skills (asking one another for information, evaluating one another's ideas, monitoring one another's work, etc)..
Paideia	In ancient Greek, the word n. paedeia or paideia [to educate . + - -IA suffix1] means child-rearing, education.
TEAMS	Tests of Engineering Aptitude, Mathematics, and Science (TEAMS) is an annual competition organized by the Junior Engineering Technical Society (JETS). TEAMS is an annual theme-based competition for students in grades 9-12, aimed at giving them the opportunity to discover engineering and how they can make a difference in the world. History The TEAMS competition was created in 1975 at the University of Illinois for the state of Illinois.
Effect size	In statistics, an effect size is a measure of the strength of the relationship between two variabl in a statistical population, or a sample-based timate of that quantity. An effect size calculated from data is a dcriptive statistic that conveys the timated magnitude of a relationship without making any statement about whether the apparent relationship in the data reflects a true relationship in the population.

Chapter 10. The contributions from teaching approaches-part II

CHAPTER HIGHLIGHTS & NOTES: KEY TERMS, PEOPLE, PLACES, CONCEPTS

Grammar	In linguistics, grammar is the set of structural rules that govern the composition of clauses, phrases, and words in any given natural language. The term refers also to the study of such rules, and this field includes morphology, syntax, and phonology, often complemented by phonetics, semantics, and pragmatics. Linguists do not normally use the term to refer to orthographical rules, although usage books and style guides that call themselves grammars may also refer to spelling and punctuation.
Mastery learning	In Mastery learning, 'the students are helped to master each learning unit before proceeding to a more advanced learning task' (Bloom 1985) in contrast to 'conventional instruction'. Thus, the students are not advanced to a subsequent learning objective until they demonstrate proficiency with the current one. Mastery learning curricula generally consist of discrete topics which all students begin together.
Feedback	Feedback is a process in which information about the past or the present influences the same phenomenon in the present or future. As part of a chain of cause-and-effect that forms a circuit or loop, the event is said to 'feed back' into itself. Ramaprasad (1983) defines feedback generally as 'information about the gap between the actual level and the reference level of a system parameter which is used to alter the gap in some way', and goes on to add '[t]he information on the gap between the actual level and the reference level is feedback only when it is used to alter the gap.' Feedback is also a synonym for:•Feedback signal - the measurement of the actual level of the parameter of interest.•Feedback loop - the complete causal path that leads from the initial detection of the gap to the subsequent modification of the gap.•Audio feedback - the howling sound that occurs when a microphone is placed too near a connected speaker, or where any loop exists between an audio input and output.•Performance appraisal - when an outside opinion or criticism is given with the intention of modifying individual or group behaviour.Overview Feedback is a mechanism, process or signal that is looped back to control a system within itself.
Multimedia learning	Multimedia learning is the common name used to describe the cognitive theory of multimedia learning This theory encompasses several principles of learning with multimedia. The Modality principle When information is in fact better remembered when accompanied by a visual image.

Chapter 10. The contributions from teaching approaches-part II

CHAPTER HIGHLIGHTS & NOTES: KEY TERMS, PEOPLE, PLACES, CONCEPTS

Programmed instruction	Programmed instruction is the name of the technology invented by the behaviorist B.F. Skinner to improve teaching. It is based on his theory of verbal behavior as a means to accelerate and increase conventional educational learning. It tycally consists of self-teaching with the aid of a specialized textbook or teaching machine that presents material structured in a logical and emrically developed sequence or sequences.
Distance education	Distance education is a field of education that focuses on teaching methods and technology with the aim of livering teaching, often on an individual basis, to stunts who are not physically present in a traditional educational setting such as a classroom. It has been scribed as 'a process to create and provi access to learning when the source of information and the learners are separated by time and distance, or both.' Distance education courses that require a physical on-site presence for any reason (including taking examinations) have been referred to as hybrid or blend courses of study. Distance education dates to at least as early as 1728, when 'an advertisement in the Boston Gazette... [named] 'Caleb Phillips, Teacher of the new method of Short Hand' was seeking stunts for lessons to be sent weekly.
Out-of-school learning	Out-of-school learning, an educational concept first proposed by Lauren Resnick in the 1987 presidential address, consists of curricular and non curricular learning experiences for pupils and students outside the school environment. The point of out-of-school learning is to overcome learning disabilities, development of talents, strengthen communities and increase interest in education by creating extra learning opportunities in the real world. In a study performed by the UCLA National Center for Research on Evaluation, Standards, and Student Testing (CRESST) it was proven that out-of-school learning increases the interest in education and school itself.
Homework	Homework, refers to tasks assigned to students by their teachers to be completed outside of class. Common homework assignments may include a quantity or period of reading to be performed, writing or typing to be completed, problems to be solved, a school project to be built (such as a diorama or display), or other skills to be practiced. The basic objectives of assigning homework to students are the same as schooling in general: To increase the knowledge and improve the abilities and skills of the students.
Coaching	Coaching, with a professional coach, is the practice of supporting an individual, referred to as the client or mentee or coachee, through the process of achieving a specific personal or professional result.

Chapter 10. The contributions from teaching approaches-part II

CHAPTER HIGHLIGHTS & NOTES: KEY TERMS, PEOPLE, PLACES, CONCEPTS

The structures, models and methodologies of coaching are numerous but are predominantly facilitating in style; that is the coach mainly asks questions and challenges the coachee to find answers from within himself/herself based on their values, preferences and unique perspective.

Coaching is differentiated from therapeutic and counseling disciplines since clients are in most cases considered healthy (ie not sick) and move forward from their present situation.

CHAPTER QUIZ: KEY TERMS, PEOPLE, PLACES, CONCEPTS

1. In linguistics, _____ is the set of structural rules that govern the composition of clauses, phrases, and words in any given natural language. The term refers also to the study of such rules, and this field includes morphology, syntax, and phonology, often complemented by phonetics, semantics, and pragmatics. Linguists do not normally use the term to refer to orthographical rules, although usage books and style guides that call themselves _____s may also refer to spelling and punctuation.

    a. Grammar
    b. National Association of Student Councils
    c. Midwest Universities Consortium for International Activities
    d. Stanford Achievement Test Series

2. _____ is a field of education that focuses on teaching methods and technology with the aim of livering teaching, often on an individual basis, to stunts who are not physically present in a traditional educational setting such as a classroom. It has been scribed as 'a process to create and provi access to learning when the source of information and the learners are separated by time and distance, or both.' _____ courses that require a physical on-site presence for any reason (including taking examinations) have been referred to as hybrid or blend courses of study.

    _____ dates to at least as early as 1728, when 'an advertisement in the Boston Gazette... [named] 'Caleb Phillips, Teacher of the new method of Short Hand' was seeking stunts for lessons to be sent weekly.

    a. Japan Prize
    b. Mondo Manu
    c. Distance education
    d. Rapid automatized naming

3. . _____ is a student-centered pedagogy in which students learn about a subject in the context of comex, multifaceted, and realistic problems (not to be confused with project-based learning). The goals of are to help the students develop flexible knowledge, effective problem solving skills, self-directed learning, effective collaboration skills and intrinsic motivation. Working in groups, students identify what they already know, what they need to know, and how and where to access new information that may lead to resolution of the problem.

Chapter 10. The contributions from teaching approaches-part II

CHAPTER QUIZ: KEY TERMS, PEOPLE, PLACES, CONCEPTS

   a. Barbara Harrell-Bond
   b. Problem-based learning
   c. Summer Discovery
   d. Super 30

4. _____ measures the extent to which a consumer has a meaningful brand experience when exposed to commercial advertising, sponsorship, television contact, or other experience.

   In March 2006 the Advertising Research Foundation defined _____ as 'turning on a prospect to a brand idea enhanced by the surrounding context'. The ARF has also defined the function whereby _____ impacts a brand:

   _____ is complex because a variety of exposure and relationship factors affect _____, making simplified rankings misleading.

   a. Abjunction
   b. Divergent question
   c. Dr. Fox effect
   d. Engagement

5. _____ was the largest and most expensive experiment in education funded by the U.S. federal government that has ever been conducted. The most extensive evaluation of Follow Through data covers the years 1968-1977; however, the program continued to receive funding from the government until 1995 (Egbert, 1981, p. 7). Follow Through was originally intended to be an extension of the federal Head Start program, which delivered educational, health, and social services to typically disadvantaged preschool children and their families.

   a. Paxen Learning
   b. Physics First
   c. Prairie State Achievement Examination
   d. Project Follow Through

Visit Cram101.com for full Practice Exams

ANSWER KEY
Chapter 10. The contributions from teaching approaches-part II

1. a
2. c
3. b
4. d
5. d

You can take the complete Chapter Practice Test

for Chapter 10. The contributions from teaching approaches-part II
on all key terms, persons, places, and concepts.

Online 99 Cents

http://www.epub207.55.20745.10.cram101.com/

Use www.Cram101.com for all your study needs

including Cram101's online interactive problem solving labs in

chemistry, statistics, mathematics, and more.

Chapter 11. Bringing it all together

CHAPTER OUTLINE: KEY TERMS, PEOPLE, PLACES, CONCEPTS

	Paideia
	Learning
	Explanation
	Intention
	Direct instruction
	Facilitator
	Backward design
	Coaching
	Adaptive learning
	Classroom
	Mechanical work
	Engagement
	Barometer
	Project Follow Through

CHAPTER HIGHLIGHTS & NOTES: KEY TERMS, PEOPLE, PLACES, CONCEPTS

Paideia	In ancient Greek, the word n. paedeia or paideia [to educate . + - -IA suffix1] means child-rearing, education.

Chapter 11. Bringing it all together

CHAPTER HIGHLIGHTS & NOTES: KEY TERMS, PEOPLE, PLACES, CONCEPTS

Learning	Learning is acquiring new knowledge, behaviors, skills, values, preferences or understanding, and may involve synthesizing different types of information. The ability to learn is possessed by humans, animals and some machines. Progress over time tends to follow Learning curves.
Explanation	An explanation is a set of statements constructed to describe a set of facts which clarifies the causes, context, and consequences of those facts. This description may establish rules or laws, and may clarify the existing ones in relation to any objects, or phenomena examined. The components of an explanation can be implicit, and be interwoven with one another.
Intention	Intention is an agent's specific purpose in performing an action or series of actions, the end or goal that is aimed at. Outcomes that are unanticipated or unforeseen are known as unintended consequences. Intentional behavior can also be just thoughtful and deliberate goal-directedness.
Direct instruction	Direct instruction is a general term for the explicit teaching of a skill-set using lectures or demonstrations of the material, rather than exploratory models such as inquiry-based learning. This method is often contrasted with tutorials, participatory laboratory classes, discussion, recitation, seminars, workshops, observation, case study, active learning, practica or internships. Usually it involves explication of the skill or subject matter to be taught and may or may not include an opportunity for student participation or individual practice.
Facilitator	The term facilitation is broadly used to describe any activity which makes tasks for others easy. For example: · Facilitation is used in business and organisational settings to ensure the designing and running of successful meetings. · Neural facilitation in neuroscience, is the increase in postsynaptic potential evoked by a 2nd impulse. · Ecological facilitation describes how an organism profits from the presence of another. Examples are nurse plants, which provide shade for new seedlings or saplings (e.g. using an orange tree to provide shade for a newly planted coffee plant), or plants providing shelter from wind chill in arctic environments. A person who takes on such a role is called a facilitator. Specifically: · A facilitator is used in a variety of group settings, including business and other organisations to describe someone whose role it is to work with group processes to ensure meetings run well and achieve a high degree of consensus. · The term facilitator is used in psychotherapy where the role is more to help group members become aware of the feelings they hold for one another

Chapter 11. Bringing it all together

CHAPTER HIGHLIGHTS & NOTES: KEY TERMS, PEOPLE, PLACES, CONCEPTS

	· The term facilitator is used in education to refer to a specifically trained adult who sits in class with a disabled, or otherwise needy, student to help them follow the lesson that the teacher is giving · The term facilitator is used to describe people engaged in the illegal trafficking of human beings across international borders . · The term facilitator is used to describe those individuals who arrange adoptions by attempting to match available children with prospective adopters. · The term facilitator is used to describe someone who assists people with communication disorders to use communication aids with their hands.
Backward design	Backward design is a method of designing curriculum by setting goals before choosing activities or content to teach. The idea is to teach towards those goals, which ensures that the content taught remains focused and organized, promoting a better understanding for students. 'Backward Design' is a term coined by Grant Wiggins in his book, Understanding by Design (1999, 1st ed)..
Coaching	Coaching, with a professional coach, is the practice of supporting an individual, referred to as the client or mentee or coachee, through the process of achieving a specific personal or professional result. The structures, models and methodologies of coaching are numerous but are predominantly facilitating in style; that is the coach mainly asks questions and challenges the coachee to find answers from within himself/herself based on their values, preferences and unique perspective. Coaching is differentiated from therapeutic and counseling disciplines since clients are in most cases considered healthy (ie not sick) and move forward from their present situation.
Adaptive learning	Adaptive learning is an education method which uses computers as interactive teaching devices. Computers adapt the presentation of education materi according to students' weaknesses, as indicated by their responses to questions. The motivation is to low electronic education to incorporate the vue of the interactivity afforded to a student by an actu human teacher or tutor.
Classroom	A Classroom is a room in which teaching or learning activities can take place. Classrooms are found in educational institutions of all kinds, including public and private schools, corporations, and religious and humanitarian organizations. The Classroom attempts to provide a safe space where learning can take place uninterrupted by other distractions.
Mechanical work	In physics, mechanical work is the amount of energy transferred by a force acting through a distance. Like energy, it is a scalar quantity, with SI units of joules. The term work was first coined in 1826 by the French mathematician Gaspard-Gustave Coriolis.

Chapter 11. Bringing it all together

CHAPTER HIGHLIGHTS & NOTES: KEY TERMS, PEOPLE, PLACES, CONCEPTS

Engagement	Engagement measures the extent to which a consumer has a meaningful brand experience when exposed to commercial advertising, sponsorship, television contact, or other experience. In March 2006 the Advertising Research Foundation defined Engagement as 'turning on a prospect to a brand idea enhanced by the surrounding context'. The ARF has also defined the function whereby engagement impacts a brand: Engagement is complex because a variety of exposure and relationship factors affect engagement, making simplified rankings misleading.
Barometer	A Barometer is a scientific instrument used to measure atmospheric pressure. It can measure the pressure exerted by the atmosphere by using water, air, or mercury. Pressure tendency can forecast short term changes in the weather.
Project Follow Through	Project Follow Through was the largest and most expensive experiment in education funded by the U.S. federal government that has ever been conducted. The most extensive evaluation of Follow Through data covers the years 1968-1977; however, the program continued to receive funding from the government until 1995 (Egbert, 1981, p. 7). Follow Through was originally intended to be an extension of the federal Head Start program, which delivered educational, health, and social services to typically disadvantaged preschool children and their families.

CHAPTER QUIZ: KEY TERMS, PEOPLE, PLACES, CONCEPTS

1. _____ is an education method which uses computers as interactive teaching devices. Computers adapt the presentation of education materi according to students' weaknesses, as indicated by their responses to questions. The motivation is to low electronic education to incorporate the vue of the interactivity afforded to a student by an actu human teacher or tutor.

    a. Adaptive management
    b. Auditory learning
    c. Adaptive learning
    d. User:Jtsstl/Sandbox/declarative learning

2. . In physics, _____ is the amount of energy transferred by a force acting through a distance. Like energy, it is a scalar quantity, with SI units of joules. The term work was first coined in 1826 by the French mathematician Gaspard-Gustave Coriolis.

    a. Relative humidity
    b. Mechanical work
    c. Heat capacity

Visit Cram101.com for full Practice Exams

Chapter 11. Bringing it all together

CHAPTER QUIZ: KEY TERMS, PEOPLE, PLACES, CONCEPTS

3. _____ is acquiring new knowledge, behaviors, skills, values, preferences or understanding, and may involve synthesizing different types of information. The ability to learn is possessed by humans, animals and some machines. Progress over time tends to follow _____ curves.

    a. Barbara Harrell-Bond
    b. Learning
    c. Pum-Nahara Academy
    d. Pumbedita Academy

4. _____ is an agent's specific purpose in performing an action or series of actions, the end or goal that is aimed at. Outcomes that are unanticipated or unforeseen are known as unintended consequences.

    Intentional behavior can also be just thoughtful and deliberate goal-directedness.

    a. Intuition
    b. Unconscious mind
    c. Innate intelligence
    d. Intention

5. The term facilitation is broadly used to describe any activity which makes tasks for others easy. For example:

    · Facilitation is used in business and organisational settings to ensure the designing and running of successful meetings. · Neural facilitation in neuroscience, is the increase in postsynaptic potential evoked by a 2nd impulse. · Ecological facilitation describes how an organism profits from the presence of another. Examples are nurse plants, which provide shade for new seedlings or saplings (e.g. using an orange tree to provide shade for a newly planted coffee plant), or plants providing shelter from wind chill in arctic environments.

    A person who takes on such a role is called a _____. Specifically:

    · A _____ is used in a variety of group settings, including business and other organisations to describe someone whose role it is to work with group processes to ensure meetings run well and achieve a high degree of consensus. · The term _____ is used in psychotherapy where the role is more to help group members become aware of the feelings they hold for one another · The term _____ is used in education to refer to a specifically trained adult who sits in class with a disabled, or otherwise needy, student to help them follow the lesson that the teacher is giving · The term _____ is used to describe people engaged in the illegal trafficking of human beings across international borders . · The term _____ is used to describe those individuals who arrange adoptions by attempting to match available children with prospective adopters. · The term _____ is used to describe someone who assists people with communication disorders to use communication aids with their hands.

    a. Relaxation
    b. Facilitator
    c. Retinopathy of prematurity
    d. Snellen chart

ANSWER KEY
Chapter 11. Bringing it all together

1. c
2. b
3. b
4. d
5. b

You can take the complete Chapter Practice Test

for Chapter 11. Bringing it all together
on all key terms, persons, places, and concepts.

Online 99 Cents

http://www.epub207.55.20745.11.cram101.com/

Use www.Cram101.com for all your study needs

including Cram101's online interactive problem solving labs in

chemistry, statistics, mathematics, and more.

Other Cram101 e-Books and Tests

Want More?
Cram101.com...

Cram101.com provides the outlines and highlights of your textbooks, just like this e-StudyGuide, but also gives you the PRACTICE TESTS, and other exclusive study tools for all of your textbooks.

Learn More. *Just click*
http://www.cram101.com/

Other Cram101 e-Books and Tests